Giant Animals

By Howard E. Smith, Jr.
Illustrated by John Lane

Giant Animals

Published by
READER'S DIGEST SERVICES, INC.
Pleasantville, New York

For Alexander

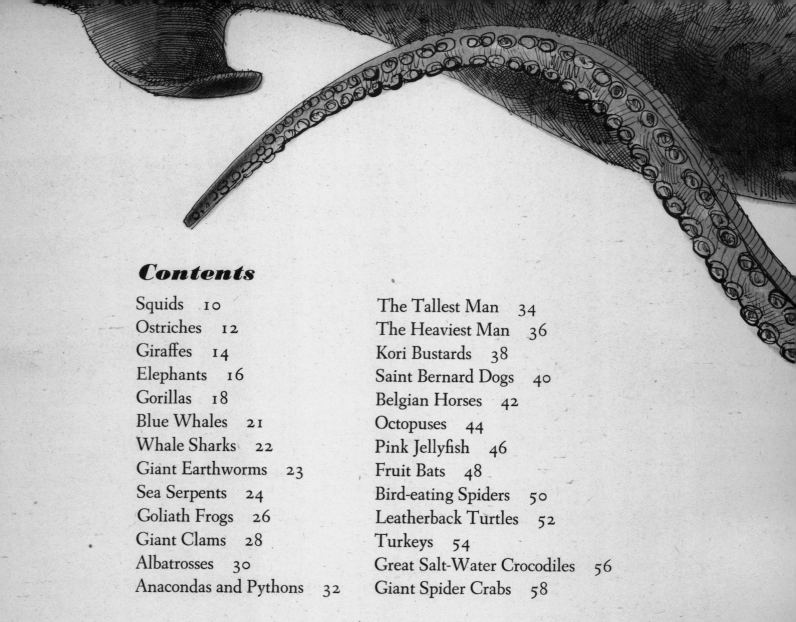

Contents

Giant Animals

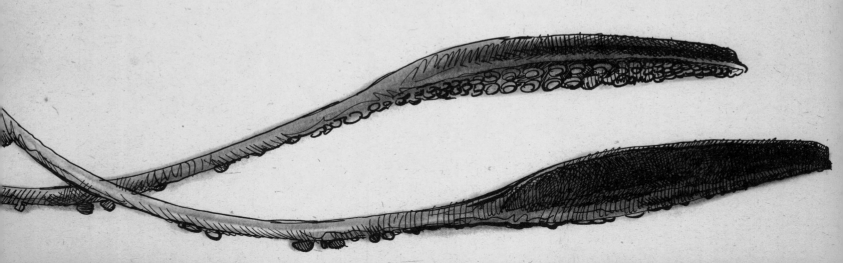

Squids

In the dark depths of the ocean live some of the strangest animals of all. The most fearsome-looking is the giant squid. With its long tentacles and huge body, it is a match for any animal in the sea. Large squids have been caught that are fifty-five feet long. That is longer than three big American cars parked one after the other. They weigh over four tons apiece. They are so big that they attack full-grown whales. The squids and whales are natural enemies. Many whales have been found that still had the scars of squid battles on their skin. All over the whales' bodies there were deeply cut, circular marks where the squids had gouged them with their tentacles. These fights usually took place far below the surface. Few men, indeed, have seen these battles.

Seeing such a battle, according to Frank T. Bullen, author of *The Cruise of the Cachelot,* is like seeing a nightmare. He tells of seeing a whale entangled with the tentacles of the squid. The

whale was biting the tentacles off, while sharks gathered around.
What impressed Bullen, as it does everyone, were the huge eyes
of the squid. Squids have the biggest eyes of any animal; some are
nine inches in diameter.

Giant squids are extremely rare. But occasionally, men in open
boats are attacked by them. In 1874 two Canadian fishermen
fought one in an open boat. The squid entwined its arms around
the boat and attacked it with its beaklike mouth. The men
escaped by chopping off the arms of the squid with an ax.

There are few modern reports of giant squids. Some people
think they may be almost extinct.

Ostriches

It is strange to think that some birds can be so big that a person can ride around on them like horses. Yet you can ride an ostrich, the world's largest bird. And an ostrich can run faster than a galloping horse.

Ostriches are big. They stand as high as nine feet tall. That is as high as an average ceiling. They weigh as much as 345 pounds. A Shetland pony would weigh slightly less.

Ostriches can't fly but they make up for it with their ability to run. As ostriches run, they can take strides as long as twenty-five feet. That's about as far as an Olympic broad jumper can jump.

Ostriches live in sandy wastelands in Africa. They do not bury their heads in the sand. In fact they have keen eyesight and constantly watch what is going on.

Ostriches lay the biggest eggs of any bird. Their eggs are from six to seven inches long and from four to six inches in diameter. One ostrich egg would equal two dozen hen's eggs. What an omelette that would make!

Giraffes

If four boys each four feet nine inches tall stood on each other's shoulders they would not be as tall as a tall giraffe. The tallest known giraffe was three inches taller, or nineteen feet three inches tall. Such a giraffe could easily look into a second-story window of a house. No land animal on earth is as tall as a giraffe.

The most interesting thing about a giraffe is its long neck. But the neck has no more bones in it than you have in your neck. The giraffe's bones, though, are bigger and longer. Giraffes often rub each other with their necks. They also fight with them. They use their heads like hammers and hit each other. Such a blow can knock over another giraffe. They can kick hard too. Their heads are so high above the ground that they have extra big hearts to pump the blood uphill to them. A giraffe's heart may be two feet long. A human heart is only about four inches long.

One thing is surprising about giraffes. With such big necks you would think that they'd have big vocal chords and be able to make loud noises, but they don't.

Giraffes look awkward, but they aren't. They can run easily and swiftly, up to twenty-five miles an hour.

With their height giraffes can eat tree leaves that other animals cannot reach. In Africa where they live, one often sees them munching on trees. They have keen eyesight, and being so tall, they can see further around them than any other land animal.

Elephants

How would you like to have an African elephant for a birthday present? Think of the fun you could have. If he were tame, as some have been, all of your friends could ride him. Maybe you could also use him to do some work. Asians who use elephants for work say they can pull a load of up to two tons. African elephants are bigger and can pull more. A big elephant weighs twelve tons. If you like to teeter-totter, you could have a giant teeter-totter and put the elephant on one side and two hundred forty children on the other side.

Taking care of an elephant might be difficult. They drink thirty to fifty gallons of water a day. If you drink eight glasses of water a day, the elephant drinks up to one hundred times more water than you. Maybe you'd be rushing to the water faucet all day for your elephant. If you took your elephant to the dentist to have a tooth pulled, the dentist would have quite a job. Elephant's

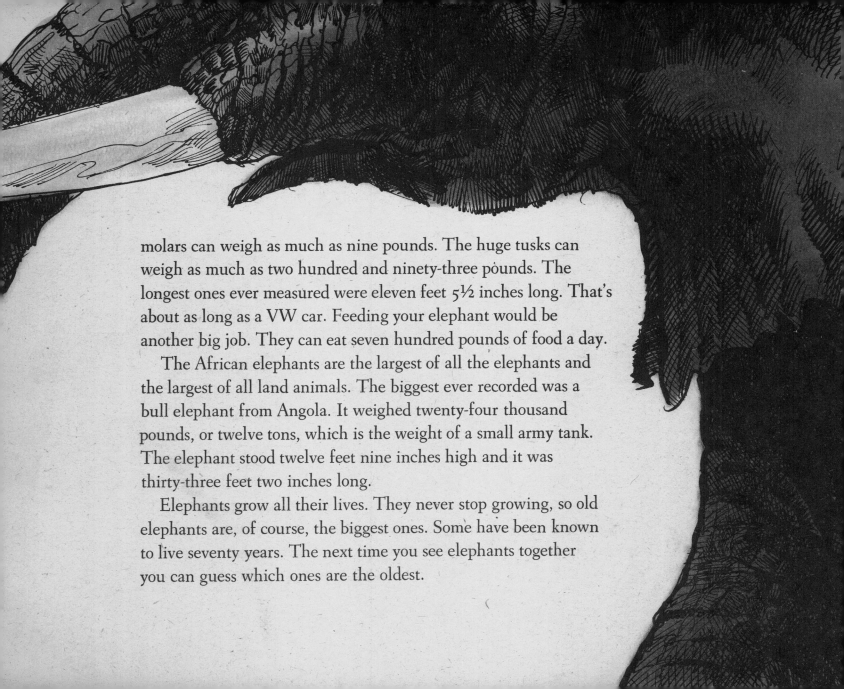

molars can weigh as much as nine pounds. The huge tusks can weigh as much as two hundred and ninety-three pounds. The longest ones ever measured were eleven feet 5½ inches long. That's about as long as a VW car. Feeding your elephant would be another big job. They can eat seven hundred pounds of food a day.

The African elephants are the largest of all the elephants and the largest of all land animals. The biggest ever recorded was a bull elephant from Angola. It weighed twenty-four thousand pounds, or twelve tons, which is the weight of a small army tank. The elephant stood twelve feet nine inches high and it was thirty-three feet two inches long.

Elephants grow all their lives. They never stop growing, so old elephants are, of course, the biggest ones. Some have been known to live seventy years. The next time you see elephants together you can guess which ones are the oldest.

Gorillas

When it comes to gorillas, you can forget all that King Kong nonsense. Real gorillas in the wilds are peaceful, shy animals. Gorillas are the biggest of the apes. The biggest gorilla known weighed over seven hundred pounds and was six feet 11.9 inches tall. Of course, a few men are taller and a very few heavier, but for their height gorillas are much bigger and much stronger. No man has weighed seven hundred pounds and been mostly muscle and bone, with almost no fat like a gorilla.

Gorillas are strong, but it's hard to know how strong. Once a female gorilla picked up the front end of a car that had its brakes on. She then shoved it into a garage and broke the tail lights. What could a huge male gorilla do? There are reports of gorillas bending gun barrels with their bare hands.

Gorillas live in the jungles of equatorial West Africa. There are two kinds of them. One lives near the coast of West Africa. The other lives in the mountains of eastern Zaire in the Congo at altitudes of from 7,500 to 11,500 feet. There are not many wild gorillas left—only around ten thousand of them. Luckily, they are being protected by law.

Blue Whales

The heaviest animal in the world is the blue whale. It's the all-time big animal. No other animal, including the great dinosaurs, was, or is, as large.

Sixteen big elephants do not weigh as much as this whale. Neither do four brontosauruses, the biggest of the dinosaurs. The largest whale ever captured was one hundred and six feet long, longer than the distance from home plate to first base on a baseball diamond. It probably weighed over two hundred tons. One whale may easily weigh as much as sixteen hundred grown men and women, enough people to populate a small town.

The blue whale goes under other names—the sulphur-bottom whale and Sibbald's rorqual.

The blue whale spends most of its time in the Antarctic or Arctic seas. Occasionally, it is seen traveling in the tropical seas. The whales eat krill, which are small, pink shrimplike animals. In some parts of the ocean so many of these krill grow that the water looks like a reddish-brown soup. The whales swim through these groups of krill and scoop them up with their mouths.

Whale Sharks

The whale shark is the largest of all fish. In spite of its name, the whale shark is not a whale, nor is it related to one. Whales are mammals, and they are air-breathing animals like men and dogs.

The whale shark is a fish and it is also a shark. People call it a whale shark only because of its huge size. The whale shark sometimes grows to fifty-nine feet long. That's longer than three large American cars parked end to end. Some weigh ninety thousand pounds. That's as much as fifteen hundred average fifth-grade children would weigh.

But whale sharks do not attack men or even eat other fish. They eat plankton, the tiny animals and plants that live in the sea.

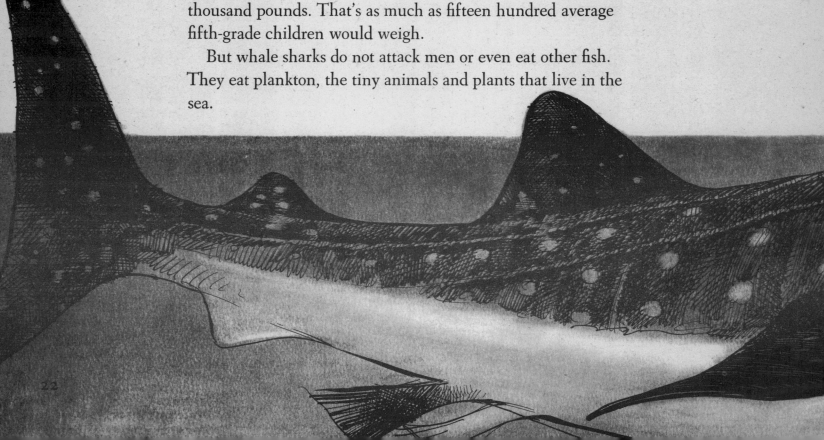

Giant Earthworms

The earthworms you see here in America can be held in the palm of your hand. Even if you take one and pull it out to its full length, it is not much more than ten inches long.

Earthworms that are truly giant earthworms live in Australia. These earthworms live on high ridges in the rain forests. They eat nothing but rotting leaves.

They look exactly like our own earthworms but they are eleven feet long and can be pulled out to be twenty-one feet long. Imagine fishing with such a worm!

Sea Serpents

When we hear of a sea serpent we think of a monstrous, huge animal. No animal sounds bigger or more frightening, but do they exist? Perhaps.

On August 6, 1848, the captain of a British navy ship saw a huge sea serpent. The animal was at least sixty feet long, and it swam very close to his ship. He and several crew members watched it for about twenty minutes. The sea serpent was dark brown, it had a yellow throat, it had no fins, but it had what looked like a horse's mane and its body was fifteen or sixteen inches in diameter.

It was an astonishing thing to see. However, many others have seen such sea serpents. In fact, hundreds of different people have seen them.

For instance, many of the townspeople of Gloucester, Massachusetts, saw a huge hundred-foot-long sea serpent in their harbor in 1817. Witness after witness told scientists what they

saw. They described the sea serpent as being dark brown and with humps on its back. When it rested, it lay out straight in the water and it was about a hundred feet long. The same sea serpent was later seen in New York, then it went back to Massachusetts.

In Scotland, dozens of people say they have seen the Loch Ness monster. This is a huge animal which people say has a long neck and a snakelike head. It lives in Loch Ness, a large twenty-two-mile-long lake.

In spite of the fact that there are hundreds of reports of huge animals that live in the sea or in large, deep lakes, no one has ever captured such an animal, nor have they found any bones of such a creature. No one has even taken any good photographs of them.

We will have to wait until someone captures one to know much more about them. All one can say is that perhaps there are sea monsters and sea serpents. If so, they are true giant animals.

Goliath Frogs

Imagine meeting a giant frog as large as a two-year-old child. The Goliath frog of Africa is as big as that—some of these frogs are thirty inches long from their nose to their toes. They weigh as much as 7¾ pounds. Their eyes are as big as quarters. African natives will call one of these frogs "mother's son" as it looks so much like a child, especially when it is held with its legs straight. These frogs are 2½ times as long as a big American bullfrog.

Goliath frogs live in Rio Muni and Cameroon, both in West Africa. The frogs are quite rare and hard to find. They can be found at remote rivers, where they usually rest on rocks near waterfalls. It is difficult to hunt them as they keep a good watch on what is going on around them.

In North America you can find bullfrogs or listen to them croak on a summer's night. They look very much like the Goliath frogs, except they are much smaller.

Giant Clams

In the South Sea islands of the Indian and Pacific Oceans live the giant clams. They grow near and on the coral reefs. These clams are true giants compared to the clams we have in our clam chowder.

The hard-shell, or quahog, clam is the most sought after for food in the eastern part of the United States. It is only three to five inches across, whereas some giant clams weigh as much as 579½ pounds. One measured twenty-nine inches by forty-three inches. It was found on the Great Barrier Reef of Australia. One can see the shell of this monster in the American Museum of Natural History in New York. Other museums have similar shells. Some churches use the shells to hold baptismal water.

Islanders say the giant clams are delicious. Think of all the chowders those clams could make. One giant clam could make about five hundred times as much chowder as our hard-shell clam. Most bowls of chowder have two or three clams in them. One giant clam could make two hundred and fifty bowls of chowder.

There have been many wild stories in adventure magazines of men being caught by giant clams. The stories are all the same. A man steps into the opening between the shells of a giant clam. The clam snaps shut and holds him firmly. The tide slowly rises and drowns the man. Don't believe it! The story has been tested. The clam would actually shut its two shells so slowly that anyone could escape.

Albatrosses

The wandering albatross has the longest wingspread of any bird.
Albatrosses, which look something like giant sea gulls, have
wingspreads which have been measured up to eleven feet ten
inches. This is twice that of an American turkey vulture, a bird
with one of the longest wingspans of any bird in the United
States.

Albatrosses live in the southern latitudes. They are oceanic
birds and spend their lives flying over open sea. They are on land
only when they mate and nest.

These birds are often seen several hundred miles from land.
Sailors know them well. It has been said that some superstitious
sailors of the past thought that the birds were the ghosts of the
drowned sailors. The poet Coleridge certainly used this idea in
The Rime of the Ancient Mariner. In the poem, a man who kills
an albatross brings bad luck to his ship.

The wandering albatross's wings are a marvel in design. Most
birds, as we know, fly by constantly flapping their wings.
Albatrosses, however, can glide for hours without needing to flap
their long wings. They can ride on the wind that bounces up
when it hits sea waves. On such currents of wind, an albatross

can glide in any direction, upwind or downwind. The birds are so accustomed to flying like that, they do not try to fly in calm weather. When the wind stops blowing, they sit on the ocean and wait for the wind to blow again. There is evidence that these birds could fly north to, say, the North Atlantic Ocean, except that areas of calm near the equator are too difficult to cross. On rare occasions, one or two are blown north in storms—some have been found in Scotland.

Anacondas and Pythons

What would a jungle movie be without a huge snake wrapping itself around an explorer? It is enough to make you forget to chew your popcorn.

Some of the rubber snakes in the movies are really huge, but how big is the biggest live snake?

No one is really sure. There are, however, two contenders for the title, and they live half way around the world from each other. One is the anaconda, a boa constrictor of the jungles of South America. The other is the regal python of the Malay Peninsula. Both snakes are hard to find, as they live in dense, out-of-the-way jungles. The regal python has been accurately measured at thirty-three feet in length. There have been reports of anacondas over thirty-seven feet long. Six beds, one behind the other, would not be as long as the reported anaconda. Anacondas can weigh up to a thousand pounds, according to the same reports. Ten sixth-grade children would weigh about that much.

Are these snakes, which kill their prey by squeezing them to death, dangerous to man? Yes and no. They live so far away from most people that they almost never see a human being. Also they eat very rarely. They kill a deer or a wild boar, swallow it, and digest it for weeks before they are hungry again. But there are reports of them killing people. Actually, poisonous snakes are far more dangerous to man than pythons or boa constrictors.

Some small boas are even kept as pets.

The Tallest Man

Giants—real giants—always interest us. We have all read stories of giants in folk tales and fairy tales. Religious books of various nations mention giants. The Greeks wrote about giants; the Hindus have stories of giants. In the Bible there is the story of Goliath, the giant that David killed.

Were there ever giant men? Long ago did some men live who were taller than today's men? The answer is no. No one has ever found a trace of ancient giants. Even Goliath was not tall. The Bible says he was six cubits and a span high. Assuming these measurements to be correct, authorities think he was about six feet ten inches tall. The great Goliath wouldn't be the tallest man on some of today's basketball teams.

Who, then, was the tallest man? The tallest man of whom we have accurate records was Robert Pershing Wadlow who grew to be eight feet 11.1 inches high.

Robert Wadlow was always tall. Even as a child he was much taller than other children. When he was eight years old he was six feet tall; at ten years old, he was six feet four inches; at thirteen, he was seven feet three inches; at seventeen, he was just over eight feet tall.

Mr. Wadlow grew so fast because he had a disease of the pituitary gland. This is a gland attached to the brain which governs body growth. Today this disease can be controlled.

Being such a tall man and weighing 491 pounds posed numerous problems for Mr. Wadlow. For instance, he was so big that he had to eat great quantities of food. For breakfast he would put away a whole box of cooked cereal, a quart of orange juice, from eight to twelve eggs, twelve slices of toast, a pint jar of apple jelly, five cups of coffee. He was so big that all of his clothes had to be specially made for him. His shoes were size 37AA as his feet were 18½ inches long. His specially made gloves were 13½ inches from the wrist to the tip of his middle finger.

When Robert Wadlow was a child he wanted to be a lawyer. As time went on, though, he grew so tall that people stopped just to look at him. If there was a parade, he would be the major attraction. In his later life he joined a circus and advertised himself as the world's tallest man.

He died July 15, 1940, in Manistee, Michigan.

The tallest woman in the world is Dolores Ann Pullard. She is seven feet 5½ inches tall. She was born in 1946 and lives in De Quincy, Louisiana.

The Heaviest Man

Who was the heaviest man who ever lived? It was probably Robert Earl Hughes. Mr. Hughes weighed 1,069 pounds.

Mr. Hughes was born in 1926. At birth he weighed 11¾ pounds. When he was six years old he weighed 203 pounds, at the age of ten he weighed 564 pounds, and at thirteen he weighed 896 pounds. When he was a man he had the greatest waistline ever measured—122 inches. He measured 124 inches around his chest. His upper arm measured forty inches.

In 1958, while traveling with the Gooding Brothers Amusement Company, he became sick. Doctors wanted to take him to a hospital in Bremen, Indiana. But they realized that none of the hospital beds could support his weight and that Mr. Hughes was too big to get through the doors of the hospital in the first place.

Mr. Hughes stayed in his house trailer which was rushed to the hospital and parked next to it. Mr. Hughes died on July 10, 1958. He was so heavy that he had to be buried in a piano case. It was lowered into the grave by a crane.

The heaviest woman who ever lived is said to have been Mrs. Flora Mae Jackson. She weighed 840 pounds. She entered show business and was known as "Baby Flo." She too was heavy all of her life. At the age of eleven she weighed 267 pounds; at twenty-five, she weighed 621 pounds. She was five feet nine inches tall. Born in 1930 at Sugar Lark, Mississippi, she died in Meridian, Florida, December 9, 1965.

Kori Bustards

The heaviest flying bird is the kori bustard found in East Africa. It is a tall, heavy bird which weighs up to fifty-four pounds. This is about the weight of a Doberman pinscher. It has a wingspread of up to eight feet.

The birds are shy. They live in the open in scrubby, grassland areas. They keep a sharp eye on what is going on around them, and because of this are very hard to approach. Hunters note that they will usually run from their enemies rather than fly.

The males often give a courtship dance for the females before they mate. The males strut about with their heads held high. They fluff out the feathers around their throats.

The kori bustards are strong fliers in spite of their great weight. They fly in formations like geese, with their heads and necks straight out. Often they migrate long distances, but they can fly only from two hundred to three hundred feet above the ground.

People have hunted the birds a great deal so that they are getting rare. There are now laws to protect them.

Saint Bernard Dogs

The heaviest dog of all is the Saint Bernard. One, Schwarzwald Hot Duke, who belonged to a Dr. A. M. Bruner of Oconomowoc, Wisconsin, weighed 295 pounds. The dog was born May 2, 1964, and died in August 1969.

The Saint Bernard is probably the most famous for its life-saving prowess in the Alps. The origin of the Saint Bernard, however, is a mystery. No one knows for sure where it comes from. Most probably, according to the American Kennel Club, it comes from the Molosser-type dog of ancient Asia. The boxer and some sheepdogs are descendants of it.

In A.D. 980 Saint Bernard de Menthon started his famous monastery in the Alps of Switzerland. Years later, probably 1660–70, monks obtained the giant Molosser-type dogs of Switzerland to act as watchdogs. Later, though how much later no one knows, these dogs became famous for their uncanny ability to find people lost in the mountain blizzards.

These huge dogs worked in packs of three or four. When they found someone in the snow, two dogs sat right next to him, warming him up with their own bodies. One of the other dogs would run back to the hospice and lead the monks back to the rescue. Saint Bernard dogs have been known to save at least twenty-five hundred people near the monastery.

Belgian Horses

Today, when we think of horses we usually think of riding horses. Because people use cars rather than wagons now, there are few other types of horses around. But before we had machines to do our work, men used draft animals to pull plows and great loads like wagons. People bred large horses specially for this.

The heaviest horse ever recorded was a Belgian, a type of horse first bred in Belgium to pull wagons. These marvelous Belgian horses are easy to train and have a quiet nature. The largest known was American bred, Brooklyn Supreme, a stallion. He weighed thirty-two hundred pounds and stood six feet six inches at the shoulder, taller than most men. He lived to be twenty years old and died September 6, 1948 in Callender, Iowa.

43

Octopuses

The question everyone asks is "What is the biggest of all animals?"
The answer is that no one knows what the biggest animal is. But
it *might be* an octopus.

Let us start by saying that most octopuses are harmless little
animals. Even though they look strange and frightening, they will
not hurt people.

Now, for our story of the giant octopus. Every now and then,
big storms bring things up from the depths of the oceans. The
waves cast up strange remains on shore. One of the strangest ever
cast up on shore were pieces of an unknown animal. In 1897
people found the body of a huge sea animal on the beach at St.
Augustine, Florida. It was so rotten that no one knew what it
was. Most people thought it was the remains of a giant squid.
After all, they were known to exist. Even noted scientists thought
this as they examined the animal. They measured the animal.
What they found on the beach weighed six tons and was
twenty-five feet around. It had tentacles seventy-two feet in

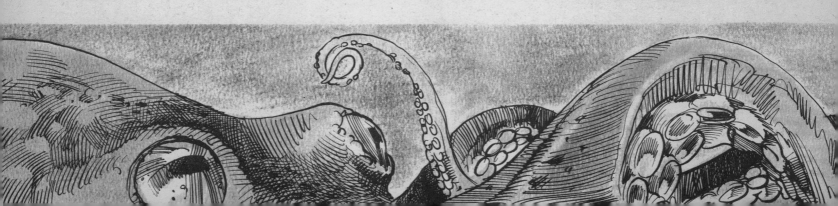

length. They also photographed it and took pieces from it and put them in jars with preservatives.

Many years later, in 1972, scientists opened up one of the jars holding the remains of the beast. They looked at the fibers under a microscope. When they did, they knew immediately that the animal had been an octopus. From the size of the pieces of the carcass on the beach, they knew how big the octopus' body had been. They knew, too, how long the tentacles would have been. They would have been at least one hundred feet long. With its tentacles spread out, the octopus would have had a reach of over two hundred feet.

Pink Jellyfish

Strange as it may seem, the biggest animal of all in length is the lowly jellyfish. One variety of jellyfish, the pink jellyfish, sometimes has tentacles which are over two hundred feet long. That is twice as long as a big blue whale. Such tentacles would hang down in the water as far as a rope hanging down from a twenty-story building. The jellyfish have eight hundred of these tentacles. Each tentacle has poison stingers. These are very dangerous. A swimming man, stung by the tentacles, would drown.

The biggest of these jellyfish live in the North Atlantic. Though they live along the Atlantic Coast, the giants are only found north of Cape Cod. The biggest are often in the Arctic. Some are found near Europe as well.

On the beaches along the east coast of America, especially off New England, one may find pink jellyfish. Never touch them, even small ones.

Fruit Bats

In the tropics on hot nights, large fruit bats fly out of the darkness. These bats are huge compared to the bats you see here in America. Fruit bats in Indonesia can have wingspans of almost six feet. Very few birds have longer wingspans. In North America only the turkey vulture and some eagles have wingspans as large.

Fruit bats are destructive. In Australia, India, and elsewhere they eat the fruits in the orchards that people cultivate for their own food. When fruit bats eat, they fight and squabble with each other all of the time. The bats also have the bad habit of taking only one bite out of a fruit, leaving the rest to rot. After that bite, they go to another one. This behavior ruins so much fruit that the United States government will not allow any fruit bats in this country even for a zoo. The government fears the damage they would do to our fruit trees if any of the bats got loose.

Bird-eating Spiders

Most people are frightened by spiders, especially large, hairy ones. The scariest-looking and the largest of all spiders is the bird-eating spider, which lives in the jungles of northern South America.

The bird-eating spiders are a type of tarantula and they are very hairy. Some of these giants are ten inches long over-all. This makes them bigger than most crabs found on the east coast. Compared to the little house and garden spiders that we see in our country, they are true giants.

Tarantulas are not, as most people think, poisonous spiders. They can bite, and the bite is painful, but it will not kill an adult. A black widow spider, which does have a poisonous bite, is far more dangerous.

The bird-eating spiders live in dense jungles. During the day they often hide in holes and under rocks. At night they creep out and hunt for insects such as beetles. As one would guess from their name, they occasionally catch birds and eat them.

For spiders they have an unusual ability. They can walk up a pane of window glass. They can do it, as they have sticky silky hairs on their feet. These can cling to glass.

In the American Southwest there are tarantulas related to the bird-eating spiders. Our tarantulas are about two inches long. If you meet one, it will look very big to you, although it is much smaller than its giant cousin of South America.

Leatherback Turtles

Have you ever had a turtle as a pet? Perhaps you had a little one once. These turtles are only two to five inches long. By comparison, the biggest turtles are huge. These are the leatherback turtles. They often grow to eight feet in length, that is, they are longer and wider than a double bed. They often weigh over twenty-eight hundred pounds, which is heavier than a large horse.

Leatherback turtles spend their lives in the ocean. They are marvelous swimmers. Their front legs have developed into flippers. With these they propel themselves through the water. Often their flippers have a spread of ten feet.

Leatherback turtles live in the warm seawater of the tropics and semitropics all around the world. Occasionally they are found on the coasts of our country, but only because they have been caught in a storm.

Sea turtles are amazing because they can go from one small island to another one thousands of miles away in the ocean. No one knows how they find their way.

Turkeys

Have you ever wondered, as you sat down to a big turkey dinner, what the biggest turkey was? Maybe your mother or friends had a twenty-five-pound turkey and you thought, "Gosh, can they be bigger than that?" The biggest turkey ever recorded was one grown in California. It was a tom turkey, and it weighed seventy pounds.

My cookbook says that when you roast a turkey you should allow twenty-five minutes to the pound. At that rate, it would take you twenty-nine hours and ten minutes just to roast such a monster. That is over a day of cooking! Next time you are eating turkey leftovers, turkey sandwiches, turkey soup, and turkey hash be glad not all turkeys are so big.

Of course, wild turkeys never get so large. Wild turkeys have a streamlined look to them. They are fast and wily birds. Hunters consider them one of the hardest of all birds to bag.

Great Salt-Water Crocodiles

Few animals are as mean, tough, and vicious as the great salt-water crocodile. This biggest of all crocodiles reaches a length of thirty-three feet. Two such crocodiles would be almost as long as a basketball court.

The salt-water crocodile will not hesitate to attack a human being. In the Malay Archipelago, people tell of its danger, as many people there have been killed and eaten by them. The

Hindus of India cremate their dead on river banks and float the remains of the body downstream. The crocodiles sometimes eat the bodies. Unlike most animals, they are also vicious in captivity. They are ready to attack anyone who gets near them.

The salt-water crocodile lives in South Asia and Oceania, from India to the Solomon Islands and Northern Australia. As its name implies, it doesn't mind going in ocean water. In fact, it swims long distances out to sea, and ships encounter these beasts far from the sight of land.

The salt-water crocodile and other crocodiles are becoming much rarer these days, as many have been hunted for their hide, which is used to make purses and other leather goods.

Even such vicious animals should be protected as all life is valuable. It's better to have a fake crocodile-skin purse these days. Maybe the next life you save will be a crocodile's.

Giant Spider Crabs

One of the most spectacular looking animals is the giant spider crab. These armored animals, with huge pincers and long legs, crawl about in the deep waters of the ocean. They are found in water from one hundred and fifty to one thousand feet deep off the coast of Japan. The Japanese eat these crabs. They fish for them around their islands and out at sea.

Some of these crabs weigh as much as forty pounds, which is about the weight of a Dalmatian dog. The most interesting thing about the giant spider crabs are their long spiderlike legs. The legs reach up to 12½ feet. Two tall men standing with their arms out could hardly reach as far.

How would you like to buy one of these at the fish market? What a job getting it home!

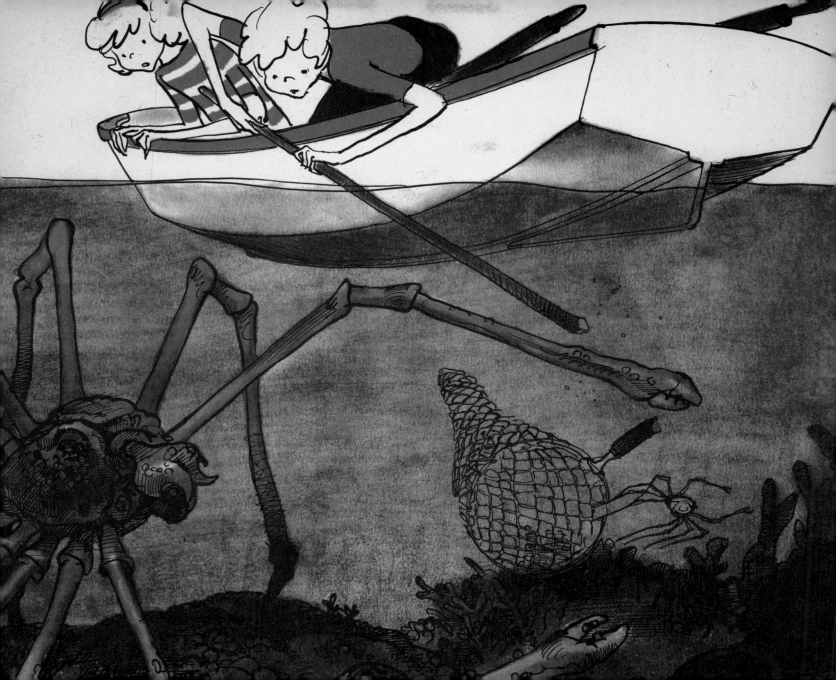

HOWARD E. SMITH, JR., was born in Gloucester, Massachusetts, and raised in California. He received a B.A. degree from Colorado College; while there he climbed sixteen mountains, all more than 14,000 feet high. He also was a member of a bird-hunting expedition for the Colorado College Museum. He spent several years in New Mexico and prospected for oil in the wilds of Wyoming. He is a science editor for both juvenile and adult books for a major publishing house and has written books and many magazine articles. Mr. Smith now lives in Brooklyn with his wife, two children, and dog.

JOHN LANE, artist and illustrator, is chief editorial cartoonist of Newspaper Enterprise Association. His cartoons are distributed to NEA's more than 750 daily newspaper subscribers in North America. He joined NEA as a staff artist in 1956 and has been the firm's creative art director for the past six years. Since that time he has covered two presidential elections, including the national conventions, the race at Daytona and several major trials, providing on-the-spot sketches of personalities and events.